CONNECT BIBLE STUDIES

On Football

Sven-Göran Eriksson
(Carlton)

Playing the Game
Performance
Self-confidence
The Good Team

www.connectbiblestudies.com

connect
linking the Word to the world

CONNECT BIBLE STUDIES: ON FOOTBALL (SVEN-GÖRAN ERIKSSON)

Published in this format by Scripture Union, 207-209 Queensway, Bletchley, MK2 2EB, England.

Scripture Union is an international Christian charity working with churches in more than 130 countries providing resources to bring the good news about Jesus Christ to children, young people and families — and to encourage them to develop spiritually through the Bible and prayer.

As well as a network of volunteers, staff and associates who run holidays, church-based events and school Christian groups, Scripture Union produces a wide range of publications and supports those who use the resources through training programmes.

Email: info@scriptureunion.org.uk
Internet: www.scriptureunion.org.uk

© Damaris Trust, PO Box 200, Southampton, SO17 2DL.

Damaris Trust enables people to relate Christian faith and contemporary culture. It helps them to think about the issues within society from a Christian perspective and to explore God's truth as it is revealed in the Bible. Damaris provides resources via the Internet, workshops, publications and products.

Email: office@damaris.org
Internet: www.damaris.org

ALSO AVAILABLE AS AN ELECTRONIC DOWNLOAD: www.connectbiblestudies.com

Chief editor: Nick Pollard
Consultant Editor: Andrew Clark
Managing Editor: Di Archer
Written by Di Archer, James Murkett, Caroline Puntis, Tony Watkins

First published 2002
ISBN 1 85999 690 6

British Library Cataloguing-in-Publication Data: a catalogue record for this book is available from the British Library.

Cover design and print production by:
CPO, Garcia Estate, Canterbury Road, Worthing, West Sussex BN13 1BW.
Photos supplied by Action Images and taken by Michael Regan and John Sibley.

Other titles in this series:

Harry Potter and the Goblet of Fire ISBN 1 85999 578 0
The Matrix ISBN 1 85999 579 9
U2: All that you can't leave behind ISBN 1 85999 580 2
Billy Elliot ISBN 1 85999 581 0
Chocolat ISBN 1 85999 608 6
Game Shows ISBN 1 85999 609 4
How to be Good ISBN 1 85999 610 8
Destiny's Child: Survivor ISBN 1 85999 613 2
AI (Artificial Intelligence) ISBN 1 85999 626 4
The Lord of the Rings ISBN 1 85999 634 5
The Simpsons ISBN 1 85999 529 2
Iris ISBN 1 85999 669 8
Dido: No Angel ISBN 1 85999 679 5

And more titles following — check www.connectbiblestudies.com for latest titles or ask at any good Christian bookshop.

connect

linking the Word to the world

Using Connect Bible Studies

What Are These Studies?

These innovative home group Bible studies have two aims. Firstly, we design them to enable group members to dig into their Bibles and get to know them better. Secondly, we aim to help members to think through topical issues in a Biblical way. Hence the studies are based on a current popular book or film etc. The issues raised by these are the subjects for the Bible studies.

We do not envisage that all members will always be able to watch the films or read the books, or indeed that they will always want to. A summary is always provided. However, our vision is that knowing about these films and books empowers Christians to engage with friends and colleagues about them. Addressing issues from a Biblical perspective gives Christians confidence that they know what they think, and can bring a distinctive angle to bear in conversations.

The studies are produced in sets of four — i.e. four weeks' worth of group Bible Study material. These are available in print published by Scripture Union from your local Christian bookshop, or via the Internet at www.connectbiblestudies.com. Anyone can sign up for a free monthly email newsletter that announces the new studies and provides other information (sign up on the Connect Bible Studies website at www.connectbiblestudies.com/uk/register).

How Do I Use Them?

We design the studies to stimulate creative thought and discussion within a Biblical context. Each section therefore has a range of questions or options from which you as leader may choose in order to tailor the study to your group's needs and desires. Different approaches may appeal at different times, so the studies aim to supply lots of choice. Whilst adhering to the main aim of corporate Bible study, some types of questions may enable this for your group better than others — so take your pick.

Group members should be supplied with the appropriate sheet that they can fill in, each one also showing the relevant summary.

Leader's notes contain:

1. Opening Questions

These help your group settle in to discussion, whilst introducing the topics. They may be straightforward, personal or creative, but are aiming to provoke a response.

2. Summary

We suggest the summary of the book or film will follow now, read aloud if necessary. There may well be reactions that group members want to express even before getting on to the week's issue.

3. Key Issue

Again, either read from the leader's notes, or summarised.

4. Bible Study

Lots of choice here. Choose as appropriate to suit your group — get digging into the Bible. Background reading and texts for further help and study are suggested, but please use the material provided to inspire your group to explore their Bibles as much as possible. A concordance might be a handy standby for looking things up. A commentary could be useful too, such as the *New Bible Commentary 21st Century Edition* (IVP, 1994). The idea is to help people to engage with the truth of God's word, wrestling with it if necessary but making it their own.

Don't plan to work through every question here. Within each section the two questions explore roughly the same ground but from different angles or in different ways. Our advice is to take one question from each section. The questions are open-ended so each ought to yield good discussion — though of course any discussion in a Bible study may need prompting to go a little further.

5. Implications

Here the aim is to tie together the perspectives gained through Bible study and the impact of the book or film. The implications may be personal, a change in worldview, or new ideas for relating to non-churchgoers. Choose questions that adapt to the flow of the discussion.

6. Prayer

Leave time for it! We suggest a time of open prayer, or praying in pairs if the group would prefer. Encourage your members to focus on issues from your study that had a particular impact on them. Try different approaches to prayer — light a candle, say a prayer each, write prayers down, play quiet worship music — aim to facilitate everyone to relate to God.

7. Background Reading

You will find links to some background reading on the Connect Bible Studies website: www.connectbiblestudies.com/

8. Online Discussion

You can discuss the studies online with others on the Connect Bible Studies website at www.connectbiblestudies.com/discuss/

Scriptures referred to are taken from the Holy Bible, New International Version (NIV). Copyright © 1973, 1978, 1984 by International Bible Society. Other Bible translations can, of course, be used for the studies and having a range of translations in a group can be helpful and useful in discussion.

www.connectbiblestudies.com

connect

linking the Word to the world

On Football

Sven-Göran Eriksson (Carlton)

Part One: Playing the Game

Lo Scudetto [the Italian football league] was not won just with the feet. It was won at least as much with the power of the mind.

p. 11

Please read Using Connect Bible Studies *before leading a Bible study using this material.*

Opening Questions

Choose one of these questions.

Are you interested in football? Why or why not?	Why do you think football is so popular worldwide?
Which sports team or event do you support? Why?	Do you prefer watching sports or competing? Why?

Summary

When you are working with top-level football teams, there is often very little to choose between them in terms of skills and fitness. Sven-Göran Eriksson is in no doubt when it comes to pinning down what makes a team successful: 'It's mental differences which will decide who the real winners are' (p. 18). *On Football* is about building a winning team by developing the players' mental game. To that end, it is written with the help of sports psychologist Willi Railo.

Together, they look at the different areas associated with the mental game — performance anxiety, self-confidence, coping with pressure, setting goals, working as a team — and uncover some interesting facts (for example, not all players have the courage to win, even if they are physically capable).

Eriksson and Railo are keen to draw a distinction between attacking and aggression. Railo sums up the right attitude: 'It is another person's performance we have to defeat — not another person' (p. 139). They are convinced that with the right mental training, anything can be achieved, as 'The power of the mind really is incredible' (Sven-Göran Eriksson, p. 142).

Key Issue: Playing the Game

Another World Cup, another season of football mania. Some of us love it, some of us dread it. But it is not only football which captures our allegiance and passion — most of us like watching or competing in one sport or another. It is big business the world over. Now Sven-Göran Eriksson, England's football team manager, has produced a book which tackles the issues behind successful football. Yet his ideas are applicable to the way we all live — with or without an obsession for kicking balls around. So the big question is: what can football teach us about the Christian life? What does the Bible say about scoring goals? What does it say about losing, about aggression? What sort of commitment does it encourage?

Bible Study

Choose one question from each section.

1. Scoring goals

In order to be the best when it counts, we have to accept ourselves completely as winners, intellectually, emotionally, consciously and subconsciously. We have to use our mental energy to step on the accelerator, not to put the brakes on; but then we have to be able to handle the forces that pull us in different directions.
(Willi Railo, p. 20)

♦ Read 1 Samuel 17:20-58. What were David's goals? How was he able to achieve them?

♦ Read Philippians 3:12–4:1. What was Paul's goal? How did he intend to achieve it, and encourage others to do the same?

Leaders: What Paul has not obtained yet (v 12) seems to be the ultimate and complete gaining of Christ that he sets out in 3:7–11.

2. Losing

A winner hates to lose, but a winner must not get into a state of anxiety about losing. Herein lies a very important point. If we are to be winners, we must hate to lose, but we mustn't suffer anxiety if we do. (Willi Railo, p. 28)

♦ Read Numbers 14:1–10, 26–35. Why were the Israelites defeated? What did they lose?

Leaders: Moses had sent men to explore the land that God had promised Israel. The majority of the spies had come back and told the people that they would never be able to possess it as the other nations were stronger than Israel (Numbers 13:1–33).

♦ Read Matthew 14:22–36. Why did Peter begin to sink? How did Jesus' response change the situation?

3. Commitment

Looking at my own sport, football, I know that the mental situation in an instant of play will almost completely determine how the players and the team can utilise their ability. (Sven-Göran Eriksson, p. 17)

♦ Read Psalm 37:1–13. How does the Psalmist encourage us to show our commitment to God? What awaits the righteous and wicked respectively and why?

♦ Read 2 Timothy 2:1–19. What is commitment to Jesus about? Why is it worth it?

4. Aggression

I spend a lot of energy taking the aggression out of my players. All a player has to do is begin to argue with the referee, play dirty or quarrel with the opposition for there to be a danger that their performance level will sink like a stone — not only the player's performance, the whole team's. (Sven-Göran Eriksson, p. 63)

♦ Read Psalm 109:1–19, 26–31. Why is David aggressive? What does he pray? How does his prayer end?

♦ Read 1 Peter 3:8–17. What reasons does Paul give for avoiding aggression ourselves? How are we to view aggression directed towards us and why?

Implications

This book is the beginning of a pilgrimage, one which can lead to a better performance, not just in football or any other sport, but in every aspect of one's life. (Introduction, p. 9)

Choose one or more of the following questions.

♦ What are your goals in life? Do you think they are the same as God's goals for you? Why?

♦ Eriksson does not advocate punishing poor behaviour, but rather encouraging good play. Is there ever a place for punishment in our lives?

♦ In what areas of your life do you find commitment to Jesus hard? How could the group encourage you?

♦ How would you answer someone who is faced with a choice between church attendance and sports events?

♦ What would you say to a friend who criticises Christians as 'happy clappy' yet enthusiastically shouts and cheers when watching football matches?

♦ How can we deal with aggression, in ourselves or others?

♦ What is the balance between our activity and God's in playing the game of life well?

♦ How do you cope with losing at sport, or with disappointments in life?

Prayer

Spend some time praying through these issues.

Background Reading

You will find links to some background reading on the Connect Bible Studies website: www.connectbiblestudies.com/uk/catalogue/0014/background.htm

Discuss

Discuss this study in the online discussion forums at www.connectbiblestudies.com/discuss

Members' Sheet: On Football — Part 1

Summary

When you are working with top-level football teams, there is often very little to choose between them in terms of skills and fitness. Sven-Göran Eriksson is in no doubt when it comes to pinning down what makes a team successful: 'It's mental differences which will decide who the real winners are' (p. 18). *On Football* is about building a winning team by developing the players' mental game. To that end, it is written with the help of sports psychologist Willi Railo.

Together, they look at the different areas associated with the mental game — performance anxiety, self-confidence, coping with pressure, setting goals, working as a team — and uncover some interesting facts (for example, not all players have the courage to win, even if they are physically capable).

Eriksson and Railo are keen to draw a distinction between attacking and aggression. Railo sums up the right attitude: 'It is another person's performance we have to defeat — not another person' (p. 139). They are convinced that with the right mental training, anything can be achieved, as 'The power of the mind really is incredible' (Sven-Göran Eriksson, p. 142).

Key Issue

Bible Study notes

Implications

Prayer

www.connectbiblestudies.com

connect
linking the Word to the world

On Football

Sven-Göran Eriksson (Carlton)

Part Two: Performance

When we have to give a performance — a competition, a match, some task at work — there are two forces inside us pulling in different directions. One is 'ambition'. This is a positive force. Our ambition wants us to improve, to succeed, to attain the goals we have set ourselves, to win. The other force is 'performance anxiety'. This is a negative force. It produces fear of failing, of making mistakes, of disgracing ourselves and as a result, of not being accepted by others.
Willi Railo, p. 20

Please read Using Connect Bible Studies *before leading a Bible study using this material.*

Opening Questions

Choose one of these questions.

Do you like being in the limelight? Why or why not?	Do you perform better or worse under stress? Why?
How do you feel when your team loses? Why?	What do you think influences teams to play well or badly?

Summary

Like any competitive sport, football is as much about state of mind as it is about state of fitness and skills. If a player is suffering from what is known as performance anxiety, he will be unable to take risks and his game will be affected — not to mention the overall performance of the whole team. Willi Railo explains that anxiety is closely connected with security — 'People with great inner security often have little performance anxiety' (p. 24).

Conversely, those who have little security find it difficult to take risks, but if you want to win, risk-taking is essential. Since security depends not only on personality but on social environment, players must work at finding ways to maintain a sense of security. Once secure, players are free to take risks — they are no longer shackled by the fear of performing badly which will affect their status in the team. The door is then open to scoring incredible goals or making amazing saves.

'Mental training is the expulsion of negatively learnt impulses, replacing them with new, positive ones' (Willi Railo, p. 127). Without this discipline, players will always find it difficult to cope under pressure and to keep up their mental energy throughout the course of a match, however well they are performing. 'One problem is that negative thinking spreads more quickly than positive thinking,' warns Railo (p. 102). His techniques combined with Eriksson's experience show that 'It is in adversity that we lay the foundations for success' (Willi Railo, p. 97).

Key Issue: Performance

On Football delves into the psychology behind winning and losing, and looks at the personality types which lead to each. We are bound to identify with at least one of them, because we know how we react to performance situations, even without the weight of a country's expectations on our shoulders. Does the Bible identify the anxiety problem which Eriksson and Railo attack? What does it say about the security they argue for, and the mental training they contend we need? Do we really need to be prepared to fail in order to succeed?

Bible Study

Choose one question from each section.

1. Security

> **By simply looking at security we run the risk of stagnation and self-satisfaction. Actually, we need the two things — inner security and stimulating challenges. We should also realise that security is not something we will always have, regardless of the situation in which we find ourselves. We have to find different ways of reinforcing and maintaining our security.** (Willi Railo, p. 24)

 ◆　　Read Psalm 121:1–8. Why and how does God provide security?

 ◆　　Read Revelation 7:1–17. Who has been made secure? What is the nature of their security?

Leaders: This chapter gives a vision of God's people secure and safe before and after the last judgement. The 144,000 probably represents the faithful people of God (the number 12 for the tribes is squared and multiplied by 1,000 to symbolise completeness). The picture in verse 9 of 'the great multitude' is the reality the symbol represents, the heavenly community purchased by the blood of Jesus (cf. 5:19).

11

2. Anxiety

The greater our fear of making a mistake, the greater the likelihood that we will make a mistake. (Sven-Göran Eriksson, p. 30)

- ♦ Read Proverbs 12:25; 15:13; 17:22; 18:14. What is an anxious person like? What is the remedy?

- ♦ Read Luke 12:22–34. What do anxious people worry about? Why is worrying pointless? What is the remedy?

3. Daring to fail ... in order to succeed

If we're afraid of missing, we'll also find it difficult to hit those winning shots. But if we dare to miss, we'll also dare to hit the winners. We must dare to fail in order to win. (Willi Railo, p. 28)

- ♦ Read John 12:20–36. What did success and failure mean for Jesus? What do they mean for his followers?

- ♦ Read 1 Corinthians 2:1–5. Was Paul confident of success? What deliberate risks did he take and why?

4. Mental training

The problem with connecting the performance to the person is that our view of ourselves will go up and down with our performance, so that we become the victims of our own performances. With mental training, we can have control over ourselves and our performance, instead of becoming a victim of our performance.
(Sven-Göran Eriksson, p. 51)

- ♦ Read Deuteronomy 6:1–25. What kind of mental training does Moses command? What is the purpose of this training?

- ♦ Read 2 Corinthians 10:1–6. How does Paul meet the challenge of arguments against God? Why is he confident in his approach?

   Leaders: In this passage Paul is defending his ministry and integrity. He quotes accusations made by his opponents in Corinth, and then challenges them. Paul seems to be saying that although he lives in the world, he conducts his mission with God's power — that through reasoned argument, he can engage with people to lead them from hostility to God to submission to Christ. Paul's application is cultural holiness. Paul ends by saying that he will discipline the false teachers once the Corinthians recognise his gospel and authority (v 6).

Implications

[Players with high performance anxiety] are dangerous, as their negative fear can spread like fire to others in the team, provoking performance anxiety in everyone ... They are typical 'fair-weather' players in that they can do very well indeed as long as they are riding the wave of success. (Sven-Göran Eriksson, p. 23)

Choose one or more of the following questions.

♦   How does our anxiety affect other people?

♦   In what ways does God 'coach' us? In what ways does he treat us differently?

♦   What sacrifices do sports people make in order to succeed? What sacrifices should Christians make, and why?

♦   What are the purposes of mental training in God's 'team'?

♦   What would you say to a friend who envies footballers for having 'made it' in life – money, prestige, fame etc?

♦   Are there 'failures' in your life which still haunt you? How can you let God deal with them?

♦   What is the difference between the world's view of success and God's?

Prayer

Spend some time praying through these issues.

Background Reading

You will find links to some background reading on the Connect Bible Studies website: www.connectbiblestudies.com/uk/catalogue/0014/background.htm

Discuss

Discuss this study in the online discussion forums at www.connectbiblestudies.com/discuss

Members' Sheet: On Football — Part 2

Summary

Like any competitive sport, football is as much about state of mind as it is about state of fitness and skills. If a player is suffering from what is known as performance anxiety, he will be unable to take risks and his game will be affected — not to mention the overall performance of the whole team. Willi Railo explains that anxiety is closely connected with security — 'People with great inner security often have little performance anxiety' (p. 24). Conversely, those who have little security find it difficult to take risks, but if you want to win, risk-taking is essential. Since security depends not only on personality but on social environment, players must work at finding ways to maintain a sense of security. Once secure, players are free to take risks — they are no longer shackled by the fear of performing badly which will affect their status in the team. The door is then open to scoring incredible goals or make amazing saves.

'Mental training is the expulsion of negatively learnt impulses, replacing them with new, positive ones' (Willi Railo, p. 127). Without this discipline, players will always find it difficult to cope under pressure and to keep up their mental energy throughout the course of a match, however well they are performing. 'One problem is that negative thinking spreads more quickly than positive thinking,' warns Railo (p. 102). His techniques combined with Eriksson's experience show that 'It is in adversity that we lay the foundations for success' Willi Railo, p. 97).

Key Issue

Bible Study notes

Implications

Prayer

www.connectbiblestudies.com

connect
linking the Word to the world

On Football

Sven-Göran Eriksson (Carlton)

Part Three: Self-confidence

*Self-confidence and inner strength can be decisive
in duels on the field, even when, objectively speaking,
an opponent is the more skilful footballer.*
Sven-Göran Eriksson, p. 43

Please read Using Connect Bible Studies *before leading a Bible study using this material.*

Opening Questions

Choose one of these questions.

What is the difference between self-confidence and arrogance?	Would you like to feel more self-confident? Why or why not?
Does your self-confidence rise or fall in competitive situations, and why?	What difference does having self-confidence make to playing sport?

Summary

According to sports psychologist Willi Railo, personal self-confidence depends on a number of factors: the extent to which we feel accepted as a person, both in prosperity and adversity; how much basic human love we had from our parents; whether we have had the confidence to take on responsibility; whether we have felt free within strict limits; and whether we feel that someone has believed in our talent and prospects (p. 44, 45).

He goes on to say that a coach may destroy a player's self-confidence if he withdraws support when things are going badly. This may result in the player punishing himself, becoming his own 'worst enemy'. At the opposite end of the scale is the cocky, self-assured player who believes he can do no wrong. This attitude can lead to low mental energy, such is the predisposition for success, which can result in lack of concentration and defeat. However, Railo adds that 'there is nothing wrong with a healthy self-confidence, as long as we retain our humility and an attacking mentality' (p. 50). Self-confidence is attained when we accept ourselves, warts and all, when we firmly believe in our resources, and when we have a fundamental security (p. 50). Self-confident players are free to enjoy the game, which is when the best results are achieved. Equally, 'When players begin to argue with their team-mates or the referee, we can be sure that their ability to perform is on the decline' (Willi Railo, p. 55).

Key Issue: Self-confidence

Sven-Göran Eriksson carefully describes what he thinks self-confidence is — acceptance of ourselves, belief in our resources, fundamental security — and what it is not — arrogance. Even for those of us not faced with a ball and a goalie, self-confidence is a big issue. We all face challenges. We have times of self-doubt and envy those who seem to have it all together. How can the Bible help us with this struggle? What is the Biblical basis for self-confidence, and a realistic view of ourselves? Does the Bible agree with Eriksson that self-control plays a part? Where do we find lasting encouragement and motivation?

Bible Study

Choose one question from each section.

1. Humility

It is simply humility that separates self-confidence, which is positive, from conceit, which is dangerous. (Willi Railo, p. 49)

There are just two passages used for this study, so we suggest following either the Romans or the Deuteronomy throughout.

♦ Read Deuteronomy 7:1–6. How was Israel going to defeat her enemies? What was Israel's status before God?

Leaders: Moses is addressing Israel before he dies. He urges them to wholehearted obedience to God in all things. God asks Israel to completely destroy the nations currently living in the land so Israel will not be tempted to copy their idolatry.

♦ Read Romans 8:1–8. What does it mean to live with 'no condemnation'? Why should we be confident and humble?

Leaders: Paul is continuing his argument that began in chapter 7.

2. Self–control

The problem with connecting the performance to the person is that our view of ourselves will go up and down with our performance, so that we become the victims of our own performances. With mental training, we can have control over ourselves and our performance, instead of becoming a victim of our performance.
(Sven-Göran Eriksson, p. 51)

- ◆ Read Deuteronomy 7:7–11. Why did God choose Israel? What were the implications for the Israelites' behaviour?

- ◆ Read Romans 8:9–17. What are the blessings of the Spirit? How does the Spirit help us with self-control?

3. Encouragement

Unfortunately, we see many coaches and players destroying self-confidence by always looking for faults and being too negative. Too much energy is spent correcting faults instead of reinforcing what is good. (Willi Railo, p. 45)

- ◆ Read Deuteronomy 7:12–16. How were the Israelites encouraged to obey God? What did God ask them to do and why?

     Leaders: The covenant blessings for obedience are further set out in Deuteronomy 28:1–14.

- ◆ Read Romans 8:18–27. How does Paul's perspective give encouragement for this life and the next?

4. Motivation

Self-confidence is intimately connected with motivation. When our motivation goes down, it can be a sign that our self-confidence is beginning to sink. If we no longer really believe in ourselves, neither will we believe in what we do — our motivation will unconsciously go down. (Willi Railo, p. 52)

- ◆ Read Deuteronomy 7:17–26. What motivation did God give Israel to fight? How did God want them to respond?

- ◆ Read Romans 8:28–39. What are the reasons for having self-confidence? List the things in this passage that motivate you and describe how.

Implications

It is much easier to build up a particular self-confidence than to retrieve a generally lagging self-confidence. (Willi Railo, p. 46)

Choose one or more of the following questions.

♦   In what areas of your life would you like to feel more self-confident? How can you let God help you with this?

♦   What is the relationship between obedience to God and self-confidence?

♦   How is God trying to bring humility, self-control, encouragement and motivation in the situations of your life at the moment?

♦   What is your motivation for serving God and telling others about him? How could you be more excited about these things?

♦   How does your life fit in to the big purposes of God?

♦   How much do your life and beliefs reflect the truth of Romans 8? How could this increase?

♦   What would you say to a friend who says that self-confidence in sport is vital, but God has nothing to do with it?

♦   How can we build confidence in each other?

Prayer

Spend some time praying through these issues.

Background Reading

You will find links to some background reading on the Connect Bible Studies website: www.connectbiblestudies.com/uk/catalogue/0014/background.htm

Discuss

Discuss this study in the online discussion forums at www.connectbiblestudies.com/discuss

Members' Sheet: On Football — Part 3

Summary

According to sports psychologist Willi Railo, personal self-confidence depends on a number of factors: the extent to which we feel accepted as a person, both in prosperity and adversity; how much basic human love we had from our parents; whether we have had the confidence to take on responsibility; whether we have felt free within strict limits; and whether we feel that someone has believed in our talent and prospects (p. 44, 45).

He goes on to say that a coach may destroy a player's self-confidence if he withdraws support when things are going badly. This may result in the player punishing himself, becoming his own 'worst enemy'. At the opposite end of the scale is the cocky, self-assured player who believes he can do no wrong. This attitude can lead to low mental energy, such is the predisposition for success, which can result in lack of concentration and defeat. However, Railo adds that 'there is nothing wrong with a healthy self-confidence, as long as we retain our humility and an attacking mentality' (p. 50). Self-confidence is attained when we accept ourselves, warts and all, when we firmly believe in our resources, and when we have a fundamental security (p. 50). Self-confident players are free to enjoy the game, which is when the best results are achieved. Equally, 'When players begin to argue with their team-mates or the referee, we can be sure that their ability to perform is on the decline' (Willi Railo, p. 55).

Key Issue

Bible Study notes

Implications

Prayer

www.connectbiblestudies.com

connect
linking the Word to the world

On Football

Sven-Göran Eriksson (Carlton)

Part Four: The Good Team

The good team has players who put the common good before their own interests.
Sven-Göran Eriksson, p. 108

Please read Using Connect Bible Studies *before leading a Bible study using this material.*

Opening Questions

Choose one of these questions.

What makes a good team?	Do you prefer working in a team or alone? Why?
What is the best sports team around at the moment? Why?	What makes a bad team?

Summary

On Football pays close attention to the concept of building a winning team. Railo says that 'it is important to understand how to build a culture which can defeat adversity and do the unexpected, the theoretically impossible' (p.101). Building a winning culture involves the spread and acceptance of thoughts that will define how each team member responds positively in difficult situations.

Eriksson sets out his analysis of the good team in an 8-point plan:

1.   They have a common vision of where they want to be.
2.   They have clear and definite goals which go hand in hand with the vision and are accepted by everyone.

3. The members share their understanding of strategy and tactics — practised during training so that they will survive under pressure.
4. They have great inner discipline, including mutual respect and helping one another with problems.
5. The players' characteristics complement one another — one Ronaldo is enough.
6. There is a good division of roles among the players — some are leaders, others take secondary roles.
7. The players put the common good before their own interests.
8. The players are willing to take responsibility for the whole team, thinking 'we', rather than 'me'.

It is up to the coach to determine how to build the winning culture, and to make it happen.

Key Issue: The Good Team

Becoming a Christian automatically qualifies us for membership of the Christian 'team'. There is no choice on this matter, no qualifying rounds. We are irrevocably bound together in the grace of God – forgiven sinners all. It is not only footballers who have to learn good teamwork. We must too, and we have more at stake than an inscribed trophy. Eriksson picks up on some vital characteristics of the good team, so does the Bible back them up? What does it say about building a successful team? Does it agree that discipline is necessary, and that leaders are key in guiding towards success? What sort of example does the Bible want us to follow?

Bible Study

Choose one question from each section.

1. Building a winning team

A team should include different personalities who can make contributions. Everything from the orderly types to the jokers, the lone wolves and sociable guys, offensive and defensive. It can be hard to find the correct mix. We can say though, that it's not enough to simply take the best players in the belief that they will produce the best team. (Sven-Göran Eriksson, p. 107)

♦ Read Exodus 35:1–36:7. What were this team of Israelites working towards? Why were they a good team?

♦ Read Romans 15:1–7. What does a good team look like? How does what happens to the individual affect the rest of the team? What is their motivation for acting in this way?

Leaders: This passage is part of an argument that Paul began at the start of chapter 14. He is concerned that the 'weak' and 'strong' in faith do not look down or condemn each other (14:3), due to different convictions on secondary issues, such as whether to eat certain foods or observe certain holy days.

2. Leaders

A true leader will ... draw his team-mates with him to better performances. By contrast, prima donnas who delight in putting others down should be put on the bench. No one wins the match alone. (Sven-Göran Eriksson, p. 108)

♦ Read Nehemiah 5:1–19. What did Nehemiah feel about his team? How and why did Nehemiah lead them to being a better team?

Leaders: Nehemiah co-ordinated the rebuilding of the walls of Jerusalem after the return from exile in Babylon (446–445 BC). Charging usury, or interest, was forbidden by the OT Law (Leviticus 25:35–38; Deuteronomy 23:19, 20).

♦ Read Luke 10:1–24. What characterised Jesus' leadership? How did he debrief his team of disciples?

3. Good Example

We know that team spirit will vanish when players start to abuse each other and the internal level of criticism rises. (Sven-Göran Eriksson, p. 107)

♦ Read Numbers 12:1–16. How was Moses a great example to Aaron and Miriam? What is God's verdict on Moses?

Leaders: Verse 14 probably refers to a period of public shame after a public rebuke — in this case seven days spent outside the camp.

♦ Read 1 Thessalonians 1:1–10. How, and to whom, were the Thessalonians a good example? Whose example were they following and why?

4. Discipline

It's important to have fixed limits, with plenty of freedom between them. The player who goes beyond these limits will certainly feel free himself but is liable to compromise his team-mates. (Willi Railo, p. 116)

♦ Read Joshua 6:1–21. How was Israel to show discipline? Why was discipline essential to the victory?

Leaders: Rahab and her family were to be spared because she had earlier helped the Israelite spies hide and escape from Jericho (Joshua 2:1–21).

♦ Read Revelation 2:12–17. What had the church got right about discipline? What did they still need to learn? What did Jesus promise?

Leaders: Pergamum had the first temple in the region dedicated to emperor worship. The Christians clearly could not join in with the worship — which may explain the references in verse 13. The reference to manna (v 17) possibly relates to the heavenly food available for the Christian who overcomes. The white stone could represent acquittal, recognition or reward, with the name on it signifying the believer's identification with God.

Implications

The good team has players who take responsibility for the whole team. Everyone thinks independently, but thinks 'we' rather than 'me' within the framework of the team. Everyone accepts mistakes as long as people do their best. Risks are encouraged, problems are things to be solved rather than obstacles, and everyone is free — but with responsibility. (Sven-Göran Eriksson, p. 108)

Choose one or more of the following questions.

♦ Why do we need good examples? How can you be one?

♦ How can you encourage your leaders? What kind of support would they appreciate?

♦ What would you say to someone who 'lives for football' (or any other sport) and thinks God is irrelevant?

♦ How can we encourage each other to keep our eyes on Jesus, in good times and bad?

♦ Moses loved Miriam and Aaron even when they challenged his leadership (Numbers 12:1–16). Do you have attitudes to others which need sorting out, even if these people have done you wrong?

♦ In what ways is discipline appropriate in the Christian 'team'?

♦ How can you be a good team player? What is the purpose of team work in Christian circles?

Prayer

Spend some time praying through these issues.

Background Reading

You will find links to some background reading on the Connect Bible Studies website: www.connectbiblestudies.com/uk/catalogue/0014/background.htm

Discuss

Discuss this study in the online discussion forums at www.connectbiblestudies.com/discuss

Members' Sheet: On Football — Part 4

Summary

On Football pays close attention to the concept of building a winning team. Railo says that 'it is important to understand how to build a culture which can defeat adversity and do the unexpected, the theoretically impossible' (p.101). Building a winning culture involves the spread and acceptance of thoughts that will define how each team member responds positively in difficult situations.

Eriksson sets out his analysis of the good team in an 8-point plan:

1. They have a common vision of where they want to be.
2. They have clear and definite goals which go hand in hand with the vision and are accepted by everyone.
3. The members share their understanding of strategy and tactics — practised during training so that they will survive under pressure.
4. They have great inner discipline, including mutual respect and helping one another with problems.
5. The players' characteristics complement one another — one Ronaldo is enough.
6. There is a good division of roles among the players — some are leaders, others take secondary roles.
7. The players put the common good before their own interests.
8. The players are willing to take responsibility for the whole team, thinking 'we', rather than 'me'.

It is up to the coach to determine how to build the winning culture, and to make it happen.

Key Issue

Bible Study notes

Implications

Prayer